W9-CNO-389

We Love Spring!
LET'S LOOK AT LEAVES

By Calvin Harvey

Gareth Stevens
PUBLISHING

Please visit our website, www.garethstevens.com. For a free color catalog of all our high-quality books, call toll free 1-800-542-2595 or fax 1-877-542-2596.

Library of Congress Cataloging-in-Publication Data

Names: Harvey, Calvin, author.
Title: Let's look at leaves / Calvin Harvey.
Description: New York : Gareth Stevens Publishing, [2017] | Series: We love spring! | Includes index.
Identifiers: LCCN 2016037143| ISBN 9781482454932 (pbk. book) | ISBN 9781482454956 (6 pack) | ISBN 9781482454987 (library bound book)
Subjects: LCSH: Leaves–Juvenile literature.
Classification: LCC QK649 .H37 2017 | DDC 581.4/8–dc23
LC record available at https://lccn.loc.gov/2016037143

First Edition

Published in 2017 by
Gareth Stevens Publishing
111 East 14th Street, Suite 349
New York, NY 10003

Editor: Ryan Nagelhout
Designer: Samantha DeMartin

Photo credits: Cover, p. 1 olena2552/Shutterstock.com; p. 5 Sean Pavone/Shutterstock.com; p. 7 Greg Kushmerek/Shutterstock.com; p. 9 Dmitri Mikitenko/Shutterstock.com; p. 11 dailin/Shutterstock.com; p. 13 Roman Kutsekon/Shutterstock.com; pp. 15, 24 (maple tree) ArTDi101/Shutterstock.com; p. 17 Tatiana Grozetskaya/Shutterstock.com; p. 19 Sabphoto/Shutterstock.com; pp. 21, 24 (cherry tree) cowardlion/Shutterstock.com; pp. 23, 24 (acorn) 3523studio/Shutterstock.com.

Printed in the United States of America

CPSIA compliance information: Batch #CW17GS: For further information contact Gareth Stevens, New York, New York at 1-800-542-2595.

Contents

Spring is full of new plants!

Many trees grow
new leaves.

They are many
different shapes.
Most are green.

9

Some look like big fans.

Others are small.

13

Maple tree leaves have many points.

15

Some are red!

17

Some trees grow flowers in spring!

19

Cherry trees grow
pink flowers.

21

Oak trees have flowers, too.
These become acorns!

23

Words to Know

acorn

cherry tree

maple tree

Index

24